The Hummingbird Sometimes Flies Backwards
D. J. Hamilton
Proverse Hong Kong
November 2019

**The Hummingbird Sometimes Flies Backwards** is a wide-ranging collection of poems on varied subjects and in different voices by the American poet, D. J. Hamilton. The poems are drawn primarily from his years spent in Mexico and Central America, as well as the country of his birth.

**D. J. Hamilton** grew up in a small farming village of four hundred people near Madison, Wisconsin, USA. Public school teachers first encouraged his creativity and his passions for theatre and literature. He began to study and write poetry seriously during his university years in Seattle, Washington. After graduating he lived for ten years in Port Townsend, Washington, where the writers and publishers of Empty Bowl and Copper Canyon Press became friends and mentors. Returning to Seattle, he founded and served as Artistic Director of Theatre Babylon, a small alternative theatre company focused on new plays. He acted in, wrote, and/or directed plays in Canada, Europe, Mexico, New York and other US cities. His poems have appeared in *Ofi Press*, *Repentino*, *Dalmoma*, *Firecrackers*, *Bumbershoot Anthology*, *Compages*, and other publications. He has won local awards in Washington State for his poems and plays, and a New York Fringe Festival award for his theatre directing. In 2004, he moved to Mexico and began teaching in International Schools. He lived in Mexico for eleven years, and now lives in Hong Kong with his wife, the teacher and psychologist, Montserrat Salazar.

# The Hummingbird Sometimes Flies Backwards

Poems by

## D. J. Hamilton

*WINNER OF THE PROVERSE PRIZE 2018*

Proverse Hong Kong

The Hummingbird Sometimes Flies Backwards
By D. J. Hamilton.
Alternate first edition published in paperback in Hong Kong
by Proverse Hong Kong, under sole and exclusive licence,
December 2019.
ISBN 13: 978-988-8491-71-1

First edition published in paperback in Hong Kong
by Proverse Hong Kong
under sole and exclusive licence.
November 2019.
ISBN 13: 978-988-8491-79-7

Copyright © D.J. Hamilton 2019

Enquiries to Proverse Hong Kong
P.O. Box 259, Tung Chung Post Office,
Lantau, NT, Hong Kong SAR, China.
Email: proverse@netvigator.com; Web: www.proversepublishing.com

The right of Daniel John Hamilton (writing as D. J. Hamilton) to be
identified as the author of this work
has been asserted by him in accordance with
the Copyright, Designs and Patents Act 1988.

Cover Art: *Birdjazz #47* by John Hillmer/ johnhilmer.com.
Author photo by Matteo Kobito De Anna.
Cover design by Artist Hong Kong.



British Library Cataloguing in Publication Data
A catalogue record for the first paperback edition
is available from the British Library

# Prior Publication Acknowledgements

The author would like to thank the editors of the following publications for prior publication of the following poems:

*Mingled Voices 3: The Proverse Poetry Prize Anthology* 2018 for the poems, 'Why Are There Actors?' and 'The Hummingbird Sometimes Flies Backwards'.
*Ofi Press* for 'If All Of Life Were But One Week . . .' (originally published as 'Shadows and Fog').
*Repentino* for 'Real Spanish for Beginners,' and 'Parque México'.
*Kah Tai Anthology* for 'No Foreign Objects' and 'After a Foolish Argument'.
*Dalmo'ma 7 – In Our Hearts and Minds* for 'Semana Santa' (originally published as 'Holy Week').

# Author's Acknowledgements

The author would like to give special thanks to the many teachers both in school and in the world who have encouraged him to write.

He thanks the Washington State Arts Commission, Artist-In-the-Schools Program and the Centrum Foundation for the Arts for past employment and opportunities to write.

Among the various individuals and communities of writers and readers who have read and listened to these poems read aloud and given helpful feedback as they were revised and developed, he gives particular thanks to the following: Laura Crisman, Empty Bowl writers (Port Townsend, Washington, USA), The Ofi Press/ Legion Bar Writers Group (Mexico City, Mexico) and the Hong Kong Open Mic groups Poetry OutLoud and Peel Street Poetry.

He thanks the artist John Hillmer and photographer, Matteo Kobito De Anna, for use of their work.

He thanks the Judges of the 2018 Proverse Prize and the Editors of Proverse Hong Kong for their faith in this book and their tireless efforts to make it the best book that it can be.

Most of all, the author thanks his wife, Montserrat Salazar, for her love and encouragement.

# Author's Introduction

The characters and voices of these poems range across time and distance, from Wisconsin farms to Mexico, from Eve to Ezra Pound, from innocent young lovers to guilty priests and Greek myths to current conflicts. The poems vary in tone from contemplative to comic, from hopeful to heartbreaking. There are poems of intellectual and philosophical questioning, love poems, poems that grieve for the dead, and poems that rage at injustice and the abuse of power.

The poems of *Hummingbird* show a variety of poetic influences including: Modernism, Organic Form, Imagism, and the idea of the line as a unit of perception. Many poems are written about characters, or in the voices of characters, sometimes multiple characters and dialogue.

There is also a great variety of topics and themes: Wonder and appreciation for the beauty of the natural world; the nature of time; the nature of language; political oppression; romantic and sensual love – often as a vehicle for self-discovery.

The poems are not arranged chronologically. The sudden shifts of tone, the many different topics and themes, and the seeming contradiction of very different types of poem are all deliberate choices.

This book, like life itself, doesn't follow a straight line, but zigzags there and here, with unforeseen twists and turns, abrupt reversals, and inevitable returns.

Like a hummingbird.

# The Hummingbird Sometimes Flies Backwards

## Table of Contents

# OVERTURE

## The Hummingbird
## Sometimes Flies Backwards

# The Hummingbird Sometimes Flies Backwards

The hummingbird sometimes flies backwards.
A girl gathering flowers stops
to watch the bird and hums a little
song of her own making
then lifts her skirt to cross the ditch
to the daisies dancing in the breeze.

Red deer rise imperiously
up the torch-lit cave walls.
Cavemen stare at the paintings.
One moves his spear
making marks in the dirt.

No one is serving chardonnay.

The hunchback hears the girl's song
and sees her thighs and dreams of love and sighs.

A Moslem moon crosses the sky –
her shining face behind a veil of clouds.

Parents playing peek-a-boo weep
with joy at their baby's laughter.

The moon half emerges from the clouds.

Light fills the window and the eyes
of an insomniac thinking of Mozart's
Queen of the Night and the exquisite
curving line of his lover's moonlit torso.

An eager chair awaits her guest.

On the other side of town an old man is drinking beer
and softly playing the accordion
alone in his basement apartment.

A writer at her desk,
chin in her hands
is desperate to think of something.

On the other side of the world
dawn washes the dew-drenched temple steps.
Inside, a meditating monk
thinks of nothing.

# I

# Real Spanish For Beginners

*A language is a whole world view, and even when a foreign language adopts a word, it usually tints it differently, with some imperceptible treason.*—Alfonso Reyes

*Translation is the art of failure.*—Umberto Eco

## Early Music

The sun, not yet above the housetops
pools its rosy light in the mirror-still lagoon.
The shops are all shuttered.
No workmen, no children,
Only chickens, bird chirps,
and occasionally, a dog,
disturb the sleepy Mexican dawn.

In the courtyard, across the dusty street,
the yellow plastic clothesline sags
beneath the sodden sheets.
A woman's voice soars above them
like birdsongs over mountaintops
resonant, clear and strong, her ballad
of happy times, smiles, a good life and love
lost. Lost … (this much I get, knowing half the words)
and the singer, knowing it is hopeless,
she still wants her lover back.

Joining her song, a child cries,
the rhythmic clinking of empty bottles,
and the rumble of a bus
departing for a distant town.

Still she sings on
with each wet shirt she thwack,
thwack, thwacks against the wall
pounding the beat of her blues
until there is nothing but this song
and the last note hangs in the air
drenched with feeling, hangs and
slowly fades away.

The street falls silent.

No children or roosters or even dogs.
For a moment there is nothing,
only the absence of love.
And laundry.
Always there will be laundry.

# After

After he goes
the waves come.
Sadness, love, anger
sadness again
in small waves
one after another.

Then, like that day
they were swimming
in Barra de Navidad,
under the Mexican sun,

one wave, huge,
hits without warning
and she is knocked down
and weeping and wondering
if it were best
if he never came back again.

And suddenly she cannot bear
her own house,
her antiques, the exquisite prints
and folk art on her walls
and the bed
she thought they would share forever.

She packs a bag
and gets in the car
no idea where she's going.

Not the islands she thinks,
maybe the mountains.

Yes, perhaps the mountains,
anywhere
but the goddam beach.

# Parque México

*for Sven*


A man looks up from his reading
at the afternoon joggers all ajog:
the shirtless buff boys
huffing and puffing,
and the muscle boys muscling
at the weight bench.

We all are running from something.

He watches *fresa* women workout,
lifting their heavy
makeup,
their face-lifts
and boob-jobs bouncing
to the tae-bo-bo-tox beat.
Their marvelous manicured nails
match their skin-tight, lycra light,
water wicking workout clothes.

We all are running.

He notices too, the long parade
of old men with young wives
pushing the baby strollers by.
The child is a candle,
a spark we strike
against the gathering dark
of age and decrepitude.

We are infinite-numbered Napoleons
thinking this a battle we can win.

But Time is more patient than the Russian winter.
and Time, like Wellington,
knows our every, futile move.

The man keeps reading. And reading,
as the light slowly fades away.

*2011*

# Real Spanish For Beginners

*"El original no es fiel a la traducción"*—Jorge Luis Borges

Welcome to Real Spanish for Beginners.
You will discover that many words have more than one
                                                      meaning.

*Bienvenido a México* means Welcome to Mexico.
*Bienvenido a México* means Welcome to Paradise.

*México lindo* means beautiful Mexico.
*Puente* means a long weekend.

*Huachinango* means delicious.
*Aguacate* means exquisite.

*Cerveza* means refreshing.
*Mi casa es su casa* means you are more than a guest.

*Tequila* means disaster.
*Mordida* means a bribe.

*Policía* means a bribe.
*Checar sus papeles* means a bribe.
*Bienvenido a México* means Welcome to Hell.

*Puesto del sol* means sunset.
*Impuesto* means tax.
*Impuesto del sol* means, If we could figure out how to do it,
we would tax you for watching the sunset.

*Divertido* means fun.
*Pasatiempo* means hobby.
*Mujer* means woman.

*Te quiero* means I want you.

*Te amo* means I love you.
*Te amo* means I will say I love you because I want you.

*Mentiroso* means liar.
*Mentiroso* means politician.

*Ladrón* means politician.
*Ladrón* means thief.

*Te quiero* means I want you.
*Te amo* means I love you.

*Boda* means wedding.
*Para siempre* means forever.
*Casa chica* means the house of his mistress.

*Reglas* means rules.
*Regalos* means gifts.

*La regla de regalos* means that a man may buy a house
for his mistress,
but he <u>must</u> buy a bigger house
for his wife. (This is a rule.)

*Working late* means casa chica.

*Te amo* means mentiroso.

*Para siempre* means forever.

*2011–12*

# The Ghost of Ezra Pound in a Station of the México City Metro

Metro station Chilpancingo
packed with people – hurry must go
many miles to distant places
now I see their upturned faces,
apparitions like cilantro
shining on a long dark taco.

# Baggage Claim

The sky, a sheet of lead,
presses down upon us.
Passengers, heavy with sleep,
shuffle lifeless feet
through heavy doors of glass and steel.

Heavier still the bags we pull, push and tote.
The clothes and make-up, the shoes to match the coat.
Like slaves hauling stones to the pyramids,
we build our secret rooms
to house the desiccated remains
of our own pale vanity.

The woman in front of you carries
a lie so small it fits in a carry-on.
Weekend with the girls –
even now, at thirty-five,
she cannot tell her mother,
"I have a lover."

The businessman on the telephone insists,
"It's business, I have to go."
Though he knows, that she knows,
about the *casa chica* and the mistress.

The drug dealer carries no bags
in his just-washed, quite white hands.
He carries only a small envelope
of large bills that he carefully hands
to the smiling policeman.

"Take a vacation," the bishop tells the priest.
"All that stress and overwork."
The priest carries only a small bag
that his maid packed for him.

Waiting for his bus
the priest struggles to write a sermon,
but all he can think of
is the maid's fourteen-year-old daughter.

He looks at his hands and is startled.
In his mind he sees what they have done.

He looks out at the world.
He tries to think of his duty
and the weight of all the sins
of all the fornicators, adulterers, criminals and cops.

In the end he forgives all
but himself.

And the writer of this poem
with his trunks full of lies
has no use for a priest.
Though he just might confess
the sins he carries
to you.

*2010 –2013*

## So Many and So Small

A movie-set perfect Caribbean beach –
cue the palm trees,
cue the breeze –
cue the vacationing CEO,
spinning the ice cubes in his empty glass.

Where's that goddamn waiter, he thinks.
An osprey gyres in the azure sky,
then like a stone, or perhaps a bomb
drops into a power-dive.
The fish never knew what hit him.

The CEO's manicured finger
pauses above the screen,
then sends the email,
closing the factory,
and a thousand jobs are lost.

Drink refreshed at last, and his day's work done,
the CEO brushes annoying grains of sand
from his long, spray-tanned leg.
So many, he thinks,
so many, and so small.

# Rude Awakening

One day, a great hole opened up in the earth.

A child awoke, saying, look Mommy,
but Mother said,
the hole is far away from us.
Go back to sleep. *No pasa nada.*

The child said, Papa,
the hole grows bigger and bigger!
But the father said, it is not so big.
*No importa.*

The child went to the priest, Padre,
the hole grows deep and deeper
and people who fall into it cannot climb out
for the sides of the hole are covered in gold

which is slippery and impossible to hold on to.
Don't worry, the priest said, the church will hold
on to the gold, and the hole is not as deep as hell.
Let us pray. *Si Dios quiere.*

As more people fell and disappeared,
the child went to the capitol, crying
to the Great Leader, Señor, Señor,
there is a great hole in the earth
and only forty-three miles away from us.

And the hole is forty-three meters wide,
and forty-three people have fallen into
this hole lined with gold
and not come out again.

And the Great Leader said,
Forty-three people is not so many,
when we have so very many people more.
So let us speak no more of holes

and go back to sleep, my child.
Let us all, go back to sleep,
*porque,*
*ya me cansé.*


*For Los desaparicidos, the forty-three students of Escuela
Normal Rural de Ayotzinapa, murdered on 26 September 2014.*

# Birdsong, Pelicans, and Morning Sun

It is a secret passed from one bird to another;
The whole of this gift we call the day.
Aurora, that mantle of colours,
is a song for the eyes to announce the sun
rising
with the rich velvet smells of coffee
and fresh bread rising.
Just as everything that is
rises in a song of its own being.

Even the fish,
still swimming in the pelican's belly
as it is slowly dissolved alive;
It too is a song.
As we are a song.
And the generals with large bellies,
and the banks and corporations, and
television are tapping their feet keeping time.

This is the song of the atom:
The song of ten thousand suns,
Kali's song, the life and death duet,
the desperate mating song
of two simple atoms seeking without love or even sex
to become one
and give birth to everlasting fire.

The overture has already begun.
The president peruses his programme
as the ushers in their tidy uniforms
hurry to seat those of us
who are still standing up.

## The Other

*Among five fingers there is one*
*which stands apart, the thumb.*—Belle Randall

Remember, as a child,
you woke one day, disoriented.
What is this place?
How did you get here?
Who are these people?
How do they eat that crap?

Their language sounds familiar, yet
they don't seem to understand you.
There are foods, and dances, rituals,
and strange gods you do not care for.
Even without a map, you know
that this is not your home.

And they know you're not one of them.
Like a drag queen in the Ladies' room,
you stand out.

TV reality shows are not your reality.
You do not enjoy their football,
or giant TVs, or huge shiny cars.

You don't feel at home
among the picket fences and happy families.
Or is it picket families and happy fences?
All saying, "Have a nice day."

Imagination is your only native place.
No train, or ships or plane
can take you there.

One day you move to another country
with a language you do not speak.
It is a country of jungles, deserts, and mountains,
Of huge, impenetrable cities, and
ancient ruins, strange foods and customs.

At times you struggle. At times you are lost.
You do not enjoy their football.
Always you are a stranger,
an outsider here, but happy.

Here, you feel most at home
as a foreigner.

# Questions of Translation
*Incipit vita nova*—Dante

**I Rules of Grammar: I am**

What is wrong with me Beatriz?
I still confuse *soy*,
which means, I am,
and *estoy*, which means I am.

To better remember the rule, I type this note,
"*Soy* is for the permanent condition."
But the iphone auto-translate function
turns it into, "Soy sauce
is for the permanent condition."

Soy confundido.
*No.* Beatriz corrects me.
<u>*Estoy*</u> *confundido.*
*Soy, es para la condición permanente.*
*Estoy, es para la condición temporal.*

But Beatriz,
what if
I am
always confused.

**II When You Translate**

Beatriz, when you translate
the small book of my life,
please, do it backwards;
starting with a big happy funeral,
Everyone drinking and recalling
happy times and noting
how lovely you look in black.

In the middle, there will be much laughter,
some adventures and achievements
but more misadventures, mistakes
and misunderstandings.

I've said too much already of childhood
and snow and cold that never ends.
Say no more of it here.
Boas, once among the Eskimo,
thought the Inuit language
had fifty words for snow.

How many words have we
for pain? *Dolor, sufrimiento,*
*pena,* parents, catholic school,
final exam and ache
and fail
and love
and ex.

Be wary of the dark and
spongy chapters dripping tears.
I once fell in to a deep, deep well
of memories and almost drowned there.

And when you find
and translate those passages,
sparkling with a pure joy
like blinding winter sun
reflected on new snow,
I hope that, in your language,
in your voice, those brief, happy
moments of a past life become
more musical, and longer
with every page you turn.

**III How to Say…**

I know that *beso*
is the word for kiss
and ends with "o" a sound
which forms the lips
into a perfect circle of itself.

Beatriz, *cómo se dice…*

I know that *te quiero*
means, I like you, or
I want you, or I love you.
I know that *quiero* contains the key
to unlock many secrets.

*Cómo se dice…*
I know the words, but when I say
*la curva perfecta*
*de su espalda*
somehow my Spanish fails
to express the perfection that I see.

*Cómo se dice…*
How do I translate the look
in your sparkling eyes
into kisses? And the
rising, falling rising tones
of your laughter into love.

*Cómo se dice…*
How to say… I am a happy man?
Beatriz,
I think it begins,
*contigo…*

# II

# Stage Whispers
Characters, Persona and Other Voices


*At the orchestra, at intermission*
*A man weeps for what will be no more.*
—Michael Daley


*Auf den Brettern, die die Welt bedeuten.*
—Friedrich Schiller

# Hotel Eden

*after the collage of the same name by Joseph Cornell*

*for Arthur Sze*

I open my eyes
though there is nothing
in here I want to see.

Outside the small window,
tall trees wave in the Caribbean breeze
and doves flutter from palm to palm.

Blindingly bright blue waves
lap softly against Guantanamo Bay.
Hawks keep constant watch.

I do not move
or speak
or even turn my head.

If I turn my head
the bell will ring,
they will come
and watch until they are tired of waiting.

And it will be the same as yesterday.
And the day before
and all the days.

They will turn the switch
and the electrons in the wire will dance
and I will writhe
and scream and weep
but they will not get what they want.

I try to remember
the blueness of the sky.
the smell of cedar
and the warmth of the nest.

What I miss the most
is the wind.
Oh the wind!
Can you imagine?

Remember, as a baby, laughing and squealing
as your father tossed you high in the air

Or you rode your bike downhill
– fast as you could go –
no hands!
Arms extended and feeling the wind.

I try to remember flight.

I cannot.

I still dream of escaping.
And sometimes wake
to find my useless wings
thrashing against the box.

I hear the men,
their boots coming closer on the hard floor.

No.
I will never sing.

# The Geometry Teacher Writes a Substitute Lesson Plan

Step 1.
Draw a two-inch vertical line.
Near to it, an inch or so away,
draw a second.
Two parallel lines,

independent,
not touching or being touched.
As if there were a third invisible line
separating them.

Each one stays on its own side.

Step 2.
Draw a one-inch horizontal line
<u>below</u> the previous lines.
And another one-inch line
across the top.

Four separate lines
not connected.
They could be anything.
They could be nothing.

They could be a family of four.
Four, unconnected people
In a nice suburban house
with three cars and a big-ass TV.

Perhaps they speak at dinner.
Perhaps they say,
*Please, pass the salt,*
Or, *Did you walk the dog?*

They do not say,
*Do you love me?*
They do not say,
*Is there a god?*
*Why do we exist?*

They do not say,
*I am afraid to open my mouth*
*lest the bright yellow and orange*
*tongues of flame which are consuming my soul*
*should leap out and engulf our world*
*leaving only ashes.*

Step 3.
Look again at the four lines.
Connect the four lines.
See, that wasn't so hard.

Now it is a rectangle.
It is a right angle rectangle.
All of its angles are right.

It could represent a happy family,
all together and connected.
in their cozy home. Yes!
The four lines could be a cozy home
that keeps a family safe and warm.

No. It is not a happy family
or a home.
It is four lines on a page.
It is only four lines
and in the center,

it is empty.

# The Pearl Diver's Mistress

You had to go deep to find me.
I was not hiding, I was not looking
For anyone, just being, being me....
Lies. I was hiding. I was looking.

I saw you but did not believe I saw you.
Saw you? Or dreamed you?
A luminous body, radiant face,
floating – a dancer's grace.

Whatever I thought I was, drifted away.
For I was yours, and thought you mine.
I opened to you like an oyster,
Every secret treasure of my being
Every shame, opened to you.

There was an ache inside me
That transformed in the moment
You touched me
And only then,
Became a pearl.

When you left me you took
The treasure I never knew I had.
The emptiness burns inside me.
Like starfish in the sun, I shrivel.
I become a shell.

# Odysseus – Isis – Osiris

And if this was all there was,
an endless journey
and each one
their own Odysseus, fled
before a trail of shipwrecks.

So many lives, and lovers
cast upon the rocks,
shattered like playthings of
rich and callow children
or lost on islands of illusion
where all we cared for
turned to shit
or pigs before our eyes.

And if this was all there was
left to us, a journey
through verdant hills, rain,
rain and fog and sun-soaked deserts
shorn of anything growing and
beggars and sheep alike,
naked and shivering beneath the useless blanket of sky
and indifferent stars in their own orbits.
Where now the rainy Hyades to slake my thirst?
Empty and lost like the many useless pieces
of myself, lost, lost and nothing but this
left to us, a journey –
long journey home and never arriving
but always traveling
together.

And you, Isis, gathering the lost
pieces of me, fitted together
like a crossword puzzle, perfect,
filled in to the last letter.
I would be thankful for everything
that got me here
to nothing.

Nothing left but this journey
with you.
And never want it to end.

## Actaeon

A soft low sound, something
between a sigh and a groan,
a sound like a cyclone of desire.

You looked up from your bath
and saw me.
The world changed
from that moment onward,
and I ran panting, stumbling,
leaping over tree roots and rocks,
ribs aching,
out of breath.

No man outruns the moon.

It was not your radiant, naked skin
or the drops of water
gleaming like jewels upon your breasts
that changed me.

Your eyes.
The two blue arrows of your gaze
pierced my mind.
You frowned, then a cold smile.

And I became Actaeon
running from the savage dogs
of my own desires.
How could my dogs hope to know me
when lust makes us strangers to ourselves.

My few remaining days
harried, harassed, destroyed
and devoured in terrible pitiless lust.

# III

# A Handful of Idiots

*Who does not long to sing in common
the songs of his own village?*
—Rinde Eckert

**I Uncle Leo** (on the farm)

When was der ever a bell dat rung
however small,
but dat somewhere, someone,
a hard workin' utterwise sensible fellow
did not stop
liftin' his head from his toil
and look off towards steeple, town or tower
and say to hisself with a sigh,
"Now what eedjit do you 'spose
is ringin' that damn bell?"


**II A Man I Knew**

When was there ever a perfect cup
or cloud, like clay that spun in a circle
till it formed the perfect cup?
– a dream container of all we desire?
A man I knew once fell in love.
He dreamt, or lived for a time in a dream
that this love was a cup;
and each day lived, another sip
from this cup of all he had ever wished for.

'IDIOT!", she said one day,
"You dumbass idiot moron!"
"Love is no cup! And I am not a vessel
for someone else to pour their dreams into,"
slammed the door and never spoke to him again.
Neither the object of his desire
nor the logic of his argument,
hold water.
So he stands there, all wet.

### III The Boy At the Back of the Classroom

Is not a student. He is
of that age and station in life but,
no, the pencil-less, paperless, forgot-his-homework
forgot-his-book boy in the back
of the classroom sits. Just sits.
And hates. HATES. He hates this teacher.
They're all assholes, he says,
for the boy's hatred
is broad, and quite democratic:
parents, teachers, kids, like
that asshole sits next to him in algebra
never lets him copy, the beautiful cheerleader
who never looks at him though he stares at her,
even the next-door neighbours' asshole dog always
barking when he's trying to sneak in late at night.
"If I had a brick for every skull I'd like to bash,"
he says to himself, and we know
there'd be bricks enough for a castle
of hate where he'd be safe, behind his walls.
But no walls here. "Leave me alone,
"I don't know. Ask someone else,"
he tells the teacher, who keeps smiling,
leaning over and quietly saying "You can do it,
think it through, I know you can!"
Again and again, until the boy
leaps up screaming, "You stupid asshole!" and
gives the teacher the finger as he storms out.
"It's the teacher's fault," he'll say, in the principal's office.
"I already told that fuckin' idiot I didn't know nuttin'!"

**IV A Poet**

Who among us does not burn,
like the poet exiled in a foreign land,
to be heard, to be recognized at last
for who we are, understood.

The Idiot
and the holy man both sit
hours without speaking.
Indifferent, like the hammer to the saw:
each works in their own way.
Yet the wood, wanting nothing, and no one,
the wood waits for whatever is next.


**V A Traveler**

Like the thumb among the fingers, the idiot
stands,
the furthest apart
furthest apart from us all,
to show us,
teach us,
that for all the distance,
the separateness,
however alone and apart we may be,
there is none so far
that he cannot come home,
be embraced,
and find his own natural voice
now restored to him,
and *sing in common*
*the songs of his own village.*

# IV

# Asking Too Much
Futile Prayers and Awkward Questions


*Ubi nihil vales, ibi nihil velis.*
—Arnold Geulincx (1624-1669)


*Nor for love, as the sweet pretend: the children's game*
*Of deliberate ignorance of each to allow the dreaming.*
—Jack Gilbert

# Questions For Eve

I
Do we blame the apple
for its shine,
its sweet and juicy taste?

Do we blame the snake,
slithering in his iridescent skin?
Just an actor saying his lines.

Do we blame Lucifer
for speaking through the snake?
What else could he do, text her?

So we blame the woman
for believing the snake,
for her disobedience, foolishness, desire

to share the pleasure, saying, ooh baby,
it's so good, and pursing her red, wet lips,
mmmm.

II
What if it was not
disobedience?
What if she was not fooled

by the snake and knew
that He would know
and throw them out of paradise?

What if she just wanted to see
that green, growing and still new world
outside the gates
in all its exquisite imperfection?

# Ars Poetica: I Ask Too Much
*after a line from Linda Gregg*

*for Gary Lemons*

A friend, a neighbour, a poet, whose hands
with surety and grace employ hammer
or chainsaw, sonnet or villanelle,
tells me I ask too much of poetry.

Perhaps this is true.
I ask poetry to speak, to shout,
to praise and woo,
sing out loud,
grow legs and dance.
To be a place to stand
and a lever big enough;
to see in the dark and into
the darkness that is each of us.

A story from Ancient China:
The master tells the student,
"Take away the words;
 words are not poetry.
Take away the music, take it away!"

"No words, no music? What's left?"

Ah, that is poetry.
To spell, to cast a spell,
to assemble the letters
is to know the secret names of things
and bring the wild sounds
hidden in darkness together,
into the light.

*Oh Christ whose name rips silk*
I believe we can learn
to call things by their right names.
Bread can once again become divine.

If on a still and cloudless day,
I say wind,
and the flag moves,
that is poetry.

# What Is Your Favourite Colour

All the colours of Green in the universe
come back to Chiapas at night to sleep.

White is a castle,
where the snow goes home to sleep.

Orange is too excited.
Orange never sleeps.
Orange was labeled ADHD
back in middle school.
White says, "Just talking to Orange
makes me want to take a nap."

Pink is the colour that never wakes up.
Somebody buy Pink a cup of coffee.

Beige is boring. Very, very, boring.
Beige shows you pictures of cats.
Cats. On the internet, being cute.
The other colours never invite Beige to parties.

Yellow is the happiest colour.
Happy, happy, happy!
Green says Yellow is drunk all the time.

People say that Blue is a quiet colour.
Blue sleeps all day and watches reruns
of "Law And Order" all night.
"I'm NOT depressed," Blue says.
"Really, I'm not."
Blue is a passive-aggressive liar.

Black is NOT anti-social.
Black wants to have fun, really.

Black is just busy. "It's Ink, mostly.
All those books, papers, magazines, and …"
Black is very, very, busy and is not
impressed that you just love the new Kindle.

Brown works hard too.
But never gets the credit she deserves.

Royal Blue just loves her new Ferragamos.
She doesn't understand
why people say she's stuck up.
"It's not like we're <u>that</u> rich,"
she says to her Driver.
Nobody likes her.

Purple is sexy. Purple is fun.
Everybody loves Purple.
There is a rumour that Purple is bisexual.
You fall head over heels
for Purple the first time you meet.
Oh Love!
You move in together.
Then Purple quits her job
and you discover Purple is bi-polar and a thief.

Red is everyone's favorite colour.
Some people just don't know it yet.

# Why Are There Doors?
*For Tori*

A middle-aged man looks down and scratches his head.
The child-proof door is a puzzle.

*I'll show you,* the four-year-old says,
with a quick and easy push-turn-pull-turn
the door swings wide.
*I know everything about doors,* she says.

What do doors do? he asks.
*They open and they close.*

Which do they like best;
to be open, or closed?
*They like them both.*
*They are happy when they are open.*

How do you know the doors are happy?
Do they smile?

*Doors can't smile.*
*They don't have faces.*
*They don't like it if you slam them.*
*Sometimes they frown.*

How can a door frown,
if it doesn't have a mouth?

*It is a very, very small frown.*
*You need to look closer to see it.*

Why are there doors?
*Doors are the in-between of cold and hot.*

# Why Are There Actors?

There is a darkness inside some
that no sun, or moon, or candle or
energy efficient fluorescent lamp
may brighten.
Only the blinding light
of public affirmation
reaches that dark corner.

There is a rain so hard and a wind so cold
that only the laughter of others
might give us shelter.

There is a wound so deep
that no medicine may salve it
but applause.

And the wound and the dark
and the rain and the cold
come back
each and every dawn.

*For Philip Seymour Hoffman, died 2 February 2014, and
Robin Williams, died 11 August 2014.*

# You Were the Wind and the Sea

*after a line by Carol Ann Duffy*


When I was young I was a sailboat
and you were the wind and the sea.
I raised my gaff-rigged heart to you.

Happy to fly my flag, I
explored your hidden places
made maps and found treasure.

I stared into your pale blue depths
for answers you could not give
and rode in and out on your every tide.

You said, I will be yours and you
will be mine, and no storm will ever part us.
But one day, the wind of your passion

was gone.
                Becalmed,
adrift, without you
in the suddenly empty world.

My salt-burnt eyes lost the horizon.
The currents at last bore me
onto the rocks and I was shattered.

Below the surface all the pieces of me
lie broken amid the fishes.
Mermaids sing my tale of woe.

The octopus curls his arms into eight
question-marks crying why, why, why.
Even the crabs will not have me.

What use now my maps or treasure?
A world without you
is a place so strange and cold

That I will never find my way.

## The Sound of the Sea is the Answer
## to a Question You Don't Know How to Ask

The sea has a story to tell.
And each wave
is a page.

The story goes on and on
and in every page
you see yourself.

You're swimming, laughing, sunburned,
with beer, ceviche, and friends.
falling in love, or out.

You're working or playing
or going to school
and steadily growing older.

Then one day a page turns,
and on this page you die.
But the story goes on.

You would have been so much happier,
if only you had
realized

it isn't really all about you.

# If All of Life Were But One Week...

If all of life were but one week,
and our love a single day,
which day could that be?

Our love was not a summer day
among Norway's isles, fiords,
and endless light that never dies
though the sun has gone.

Our love was not a winter day,
cozy and warm by the fire;
happily snowed in, nothing to do,
no place to go, and no one we cared to see.

Our love was not a payday,
despite the obvious rewards
after long patient waiting
and incomprehensible withholdings.

Our love was not a national holiday,
despite the noisy nocturnal celebrations,
the fireworks, the oft repeated pledges
and periodic declarations of independence.

Our love seemed like the first day of school.
We shivered like school children,
in anticipation of all we would soon discover,
smiling and proud of our shiny new things.

But no, our love was not
the first day of school
though there were hard lessons learned,
and many pencils broken.

Our love was this:
A fog-bound day in a sleepy seaport town,
with empty wharves waiting
for boats that never came

and the low moans of foghorns from
passing ships we could never see.
The damp cold cut through every coat,
freezing our flesh as if naked.

Faint light, neither day nor night,
casting shadows in the fog. Shadows
that were never what we imagined them to be.

# Is It Days You Keep

*I need a calendar on this table*, you said,
*I like to keep my days under my hand.*

Is it days you keep,
there at arm's-length, or nights?

The awkward silence floated in the room
like a black hair in a cream soup.

I want to kiss you,
I wanted to say, but could not.
I stared at the curving cartilage of your ear
– a soft-fleshed seashell curling into itself.

I wanted to say…
but the sound of fishermen eating oysters
suddenly filled my mind.

I wanted to say
that I feared falling in love
and needing you
more than I could bear to need;
that love is the mirror we end up running from,
unable to forget what we've seen.
For love reveals not the beloved,
but ourselves,
in all our terrible beauty, cruelty, and fear.

The awkward pause persisted.
Wallenda! I blurted out,
or the wine blurted out,
Wallenda walks the tightrope without a net!
Lindbergh, Amelia Earhart, people take crazy chances!

What if we were strong enough
to only say what we really feel?
*The day I come to that
I know I'm sinking,* you said.

Like the wineglass we drowned in the dishpan
rose refilled, so too will I sink,
or fall, if you'll fall with me,
into whatever comes next.

*Winter comes next,* you say, *and rain.*

On the porch is a bucket
filled with stars' reflections.
We'll throw it into the sky
and make new stars to shine
when the others
are covered
with clouds.

# Haiku: I Miss You, Sometimes

Long car trips alone
Radio blares, but no one
Critiques my singing.

# Meeting Again After a Long Time

Her face was winter,
her eyes, ice. I don't
miss you, I miss the
we, that we once were.

# Modern Love

In love, and young, they stroll the moonlit beach.
So like a TV show, her left hand holds
his right, their copper-coloured skin aglow,
their muscled thighs with every footstep flex.
Each falling wave repeats polite applause.
Oh how do they resist the siren call
of hormones blazing in their blood and loins?
He must feel his pounding heart, his burning
urge to kiss her trembling lips, perfect mouth,
and pull her lovely body close to his?
I forget myself. Ahh, to be so young,
but no. These two, so innocent, they touch
only hand to hand and smile and murmur
softly, each into their separate cell phones.

*Zihuatanejo – 2012*

# After a Foolish Argument

The blackberry does not choose the thorns
nor does it ask
your forgiveness.

Only that you be filled with grace
as finches filled with grace and song
move unscathed among thorns.

Or that you endure them
as the bears endure,
indifferent to the thousand cuts;

Bellies full of juicy, sweet berries,
their thick black fur, wet and
glistening like lovers after loving.

# V

# Semana Santa
# (Holy Week)

# Semana Santa (Holy Week)

## Palm Sunday

*Lay down the palm fronds, the branches,*
*lay down green vestments*
*stripped from the trees,*
*lay down greenbacks*
*peeled like leaves from artichokes.*
*Lay down the green lives of young men,*
*lay down the ripe as well.*
*The Saviour, the Saviour, El Salvador*
*comes riding on the bodies of its children*
*and a cold, cold wind from the North.*

It is Palm Sunday and raining
on Bainbridge Island.
Archbishop Romero is three years dead.
*Introibo ad altare Dei.*
Slain in the chapel
as he faced his assassins
with the wide open eyes of a child.
A lamb before a pack of dogs.
But not dogs, no....
What kind of creatures are these?
Did they salivate
in the instant before the kill
dreaming of American money
and the whores and the liquor it would buy?

Was it months in the planning,
or was it his sermon on the radio
the day before that set them off?
He dared to speak of atrocities,

Was it politics as usual that morning?

Did they kiss their wives with tender lips
that morning? Make love? Did they come?
Did they come into the church crossing themselves,
"In nomine patris," under their breath?
Were their fingers still moist
as they pulled the triggers – March 24, 1980 –
and Romero at last lay down and was still.
Did they look at him then without emotion?

The temple of the body, to them
no more than rags seeping blood.

I say this not to shock you.
It gives me no joy
to conjure an old priest's ghost.
I'd rather make love
or read and drink coffee all day long
but every awful drop of cream
writhes in my cup, the clouds rising
in the shape of a dead man's face.


**Last Supper**
*There are some for whom the cock cannot crow
without hearing Peter denounce his Lord.*—Jim Heynen

Existential dramas,
our petty crises of faith
are nothing to the rooster.

No matter that the ax
was sharpened yesterday,
that the farmer is drunk
and sleeping it off, that humans
are notorious for bad tempers.
No matter to one whose voice
sends vampires into hiding.

Each day the farmer rises
may be the end but still
the rooster bravely
flies to the rooftop
turns his fishy eye to the East
and sings the world awake
with his noisy, unpleasant, political poem.


**Good Friday**

In a jungle
in a quiet room,
where the floor
whispers every footstep,
the nurses in nuns' habits –
white cloth clouds float.
I never see their feet.

The priest keeps vigil
beside a mass of bandages and
burned flesh that once was a kid,
a skinny fifteen-year-old soldier
who didn't seem to mind the killing.
And next to him
one left for dead in a ditch
left without fingers
without flesh or feeling
between the legs, broken legs.
Eyeless, as blind as –
no – not justice, that's a lie.
Only grace is blind.

The priest anoints them
both with oil, prays
and kisses the stole
and puts it away

and one of them dies.
Which, I don't recall.

Which of the thieves was saved?


**Holy Saturday**
*"I greatly fear that very soon the Bible will not be allowed
in our country ... because all of the pages are subversive.*
—Father Rutilio Grande, S.J., assassinated in El Salvador,
1977.


Outside the gates of the embassy
the colours of dawn unravel and fade.
The day opens itself like a gift
of stale bread wrapped in bright paper.
The priest recalls a Wisconsin sunrise,
the cow's warm teats in his hands,
long walks to school, teasing Jerry
and standing to recite memorized prayers
and lists. THE SINS WHICH CRY TO HEAVEN
FOR VENGENCE: Willful murder, rape,
oppression of the poor, the widows, and orphans,
defrauding labourers of their just wages.

He missed Jerry. The obituary said only
Father Jerome Cypher, died June 25, 1975, Juticalpa.
Nothing about the Honduran security forces,
the public beating, or the castrated, gunshot corpse.

He had seen the cruel women,
cruel men, ignoring the dead,
smoking cigarettes with hard thin lips
as nearby, people were dying.
The embassy office fluorescent lights
reflected in their shining shoes,
but in their faces, nothing, not even lies.

*There are also sins committed*
*by neglecting the duties of ones state of life.*
The priest stares at the flagpole,
reminded of a cigarette, wishing he'd quit.
Everyone's secret name is Desire.

A breeze lifts the flag
like a storm cloud across the sun
and a shadow falls over the priest.
Two American military advisors walk by,
names written on their chests.


**Easter Sunday**

Easter in the forest finds
Michael a smiling Saint Francis,
beatific, and undisturbed by survey stakes,
road crews and his own eviction notice.
He gathers flowers from the bulldozer's path:
Trillium, orchids, wild daffodils swaying
like mad dancers before the firing squad –
Progress, Order, Wider Roads!

*Knock down the outhouse,*
*blow out the kerosene lamps.*
Electricity's true name is power.

The landless, the squatters, refugiados;
the meek, Michael, will inherit nothing,
not the Earth, not any part of it,
not the holes they dump the bodies into,
not this broken dirt road leading – where? To what?
These questions hang
useless as tuxedos in a hungry man's closet.

We stare out the cabin window
at the mute face of the sea,
the toothed mountains
and sunset bleeding across the sky.
Looking for something we can take with us?
I don't know Michael.
What were you looking for
in those dark remote planets
that are the eyes of Salvadorans?
I saw nothing, less than nothing.
I saw myself, weak and scared,
running from deportation, desperate,
homeless, stealing and stolen from, afraid.

How can we help them?
How can we not?
Duty is a word learned in childhood.
Easter Duty. Communion. Pass the bread.
*Sacra Hostia* – Holy victim.
Yes there are hostages.
You see the victims, the refugees.
If we deny them we deny ourselves.

If not ourselves, who are we?
No saviour rises bathed in light
but that we must raise him
from the cold tomb of our own hearts.
A hand extended,
bread to the hungry,
refuge,
rolls back the stone from the tomb.

Let the women go forth to the villages,
let the women in one voice announce,
"La gente, the people, have risen".

*1983–1986*

# VI

# In Ruins

The Mayans, the Leaf-cutter Ants and the Wheel of Time

**I No Foreign Objects**

Unlike us
a pencil, a wristwatch, a cup,
even Odysseus' oar
planted upright in the earth;
No thing
is truly foreign.
Left in any country long enough
objects pull on their coats of dust
with perfect equanimity.

Time is the currency
with which an object buys a place.
In a country where no one salts their meat
Odysseus' oar has weathered and been bleached
in turn by rain and sun. The oar
(unknown by that name)
does not miss the sea.
Here it is the measure of snow,
silent witness, and everyone's memory
of fierce, unforgiving Januarys.

And what of us,
whom no amount of time or dust
can release from stubborn individuality
or enfold in warm arms of belonging.
Exiles, transplants, foreigners,
home was not a room to simply
close a door and walk away from.
And the path we are on
will never take us there again.

**II Palenque**

Descend
into darkness,
descend into silence
descend into absence of space
and air. Step by step
the dark passage narrows.
Like ants, we crawl through the tunnels
of a vast underground kingdom.

At the end of the steps of the temple
of the dead king wearing jade
                          I stop.
Paralyzed by the beauty and the power
of death in the belly of the pyramid.
This silence is more than the absence of sound.
It is cobwebs in a dead man's mouth,
snake scales sliding over ancient stones
and humid stale air that never moves.
It is the sound of flesh abandoning the skeleton.

I stare into the tomb,
unable to resist its spell.
A minute passes, or an hour?

Can the living truly know time?
We see only that wheel of illusion,
the clock,
that makes us time's plaything.

What is a day? Precious cargo.
To the Maya a day is *Kin.*
Twenty days is *Uinal,* eighteen *uinal* is 360 *kin.*
Eighteen *uinal* plus five empty *kin*
marks one full trip of the earth
around the sun – a *tun.*

To the Maya time is a sacred burden.
And each day, a living god,
marching in a great parade.
Each bears the weight of the greater gods
balanced upon them,
like acrobats in a human pyramid.

So each *kin* (day) in turn carries
his share of the weight as twenty *kin* carry the *uinal*.
And the eighteen gods of the weeks
all bear the *tun* and twenty *tun*
carry the *katun*
and upward to the *baktun*
in this never ending parade
like a giant pyramid of marching, dancing,
inexhaustible, acrobat-gods
in time's never-ending procession.

Only the dead know the immensity
of all things beyond the wristwatch.


**III Tikal**

Among the timeless treasures of Tikal
an endless march of leaf-cutter ants,
each one with precious cargo –
parades to their Queen,
bearing a jade green gift.

Like long, long lines of students
bearing homework,
more than any teacher can digest.

## IV Last Candle

The gods of Tikal are dead;
Let the new gods pass away as well.
Let every cathedral's shining steeple
every glittering dome, every
synagogue, temple, münster,
mosque, and meeting house
stand empty and
abandoned
in silent testament
to the folly of man.

Let churches all wear weeds as vestments
and mosses grow, different mosses,
green and deep, to carpet the steps.
Let spider-webs drape the broken windows
and wind be the only hymn.

When the very last candle
is all burned away
and every bell is ribboned in rust,
the last true believer has turned into dust
then no one will enter, and no one will pray
or curse their neighbour, or poke out an eye
or cut off a limb for some perceived sin.
And none will be beaten because of a creed
And none will be damned for what they believe.

Then peace will come to Earth at last,
unmarked by any song or dance

only a final procession
of ants.

## V Numbers

The largest and most complex
non-human societies on Earth
inhabit the Americas, forming
underground cities that extend thirty metres across,
with smaller suburbs extending out
to a radius of eighty metres.
As many as eight million
may live in one giant ant-metropolis.
Up to 1.8 million ants in one colony
may be named "Jimmy."

The Leaf-cutter ants' amazingly powerful.
jaws vibrate a thousand times a second
to slice through leaves and stems. They carry
bits of leaf that weigh twenty times their own weight.
No ant colony has ever been found
to contain a fitness centre.

None of the forty-plus species of leaf-cutter ants
(genera *Atta* and *Acromyrmex)*
eat the leaves; rather,
they are shredded and mixed with secretions
from the ants' bodies to produce a compost.
Leucoagaricus gongylophorus –
a type of fungus – grows from this compost.
The ants feed on this fungus.

Highly evolved to harvest leaves
in order to feed their fungal crop,
the ants are true farmers.
Nine species have evolved the ability
to complain about the weather and
to apply for Federal agriculture subsidies.

**VI Poco a Poco**

Among the many dead gods of Tikal,
the endless march of ants murders a tree,
one fraction of a leaf at a time.

So it comes to us.
Like a smoker's one little cough,
the fat man's extra pound, or
the silent mutation of a single cell;
as subtle, as harmless, as relentless
and as final
as ants.


**VII A List**

The leaf-cutter ant makes a list.
At the top of the page
the ant writes, "To Do."
1. Walk to the tree
2. Tear off a bit of leaf
3. Take leaf back to nest

4. Walk to the tree
5. Tear off a bit of leaf
6. Take leaf back to nest.
7. Walk to the tree
8. Tear off a bit of leaf
9. Take leaf back to nest.

10. Walk to the tree
11. Tear off a bit of leaf
12. Take leaf back to nest.

The list continues.
Stupid ants!
You laugh at their list.

You finish your coffee.
You go to your office.
You do your work.
You come back home.
Just like you did yesterday.


**VIII Monkey**

The tree-top monkey's desperate howls
echo from the ancient stones of Tikal,
While the ants march single-minded,
and silent as Trappist Monks.

The males claim territory, assert ego
and manifest their dominance
through howls and shrieks and fast
cars, pyramids, and guns.
The ancient, eternal,
"Hey baby, wanna hang out?"

Marching on in noiseless toil, the ants
Voice no frustration or pleasure or pain.
They reproduce with assembly-line efficiency,
and sexless, corporate zeal.
One ant dies, one hundred hatch,
and the business of accumulating green,
is unhindered by grief, or joy, or regret.

The Monkey population declines.
One day, no doubt, extinct.

These stones
and the ants,
will remain.


**IX At the Edge**

Seated at the edge of the steps
of the temple of the dead
King Jaguar Paw, I see
a wide-eyed child, no more than seven,
mouth agape in uncontainable excitement
pull away from his mother's hand

and run full out for the pyramid steps.
"No," she barks, "No," again as she
chases him down and seizes his hand,
"You can't go up there by yourself."
Seven years old is Australia. Or rather
it is like Australia, but smaller.

Seven is an island in the Ocean of No.
The coolest place to ride your bike,
the store with all the shiny things.
All wishes and dreams, and places you want to go
lie just beyond the Ocean of No.
Wait, they tell you, wait.

You wait, like Hamlet at a traffic light,
And wait and think and wait and
Then the light changes at last
from red to red.

Young Stephan Dedalus
imagines, that when he is old,
he will remember himself as a young man
who imagined himself old, and think,

as old men do of how they used to
imagine themselves in another time.

A gringo selling pot pipes and feathers
calls himself "shaman," lights incense
and chants, "Solstice 2012,
the Mayan Calendar, and the end of the world."

He says he's discovered the end of time.
With his back-of-the-cereal-box, made for TV
pseudo-science. He couldn't discover
the end of a bicycle chain.

Wheels within wheels within wheels spin.
This isn't the end,
just the shifting of the gears.


**X Colour and Line and the Way**

Every day, every possible angle,
I search, yet never see them. Suddenly,
like miniature rainbows, the toucans
splash vibrant colours across the azure sky,
an instant of beauty,
now just as suddenly vanished
into the jungle canopy,
like some mythic empire
existing only in a poem.

On the rainforest floor, the ants,
are an endless march of monochrome.
Their colony was old
before the first Mayan King
transformed stones into pyramids
in perfect alignment with the stars.
A futile claim of immortality.

Each ant in this eternal parade
is a point in an infinite line.
The Mother of Mayan Geometry.
Tireless as time,
as the ancient, innumerable stars,
as the ever moving Tao.

# CODA

# Absolution

# Forgive Us Our Trespasses

I
No one escapes the little prison called childhood.
Memory revokes your parole and
You are back among the bullies
and the blows and shaming nuns
swooping down like huge black birds
from unseen heights to torment you

with beatings and humiliations.
Again, the echo of daily mass
mumbled in low-voiced lethargic Latin.
Again the terror of the little box,
the screen slides back in the dark
and the old priest's alcoholic breath…

*How long since your last confession?*

II
Only at the beach do I not feel trapped.
Here among the tide pools
where everything is nebulous
One cannot say that this
belongs to the land, or to the sea.
A part of both, ruled by neither.

This is the holy place.
The gulls crying chorus
after chorus of never ending Kyries
in the cathedral of sky
and the bonfire's smoky incense
smelling of seaweed and salt.
Twice daily the high tide rises
to wash away our trespasses.

The natural, unmarked beach restored.
There is no penance
left in me to say.
Here at the edge of *known* and *unknown,*
I stand without a cross or a candle,
before the freedom of the endless horizon.


III
By the power of the bottomless sea
and all its fishes,
I absolve you.
And bless you, in the name of the sea,
the whales and birds of the air.

I bid you go in peace,
With compassion for all living things.
Walk mindfully upon this good green earth
the maker and giver of all life.

May all selfishness
and all the evil deeds of your life
pass away
like befouled smoke
before the cleansing wind.

And may the good you do for others
live on
long after our bodies
are food for the worms
and our names
are washed away in the rain.

# Notes on the Poems

I

**Parque México**
*fresa* – 1. (lit.) strawberry; 2. Mexican slang for a rich person, especially a spoiled child of the very rich.

**Real Spanish for Beginners**
*El original no es fiel a la traducción.* – The original is not faithful to the translation.
*Puente* – 1. (lit.) bridge; 2. Mexican slang for a three- or four-day weekend.
*huachinango* – Red Snapper
*mordida* – 1. (lit.) a small bite. 2. a bribe.
*Checar sus papeles* – Check your papers.
*casa chica* – 1. (lit.) small house; 2. Mexican slang for the house of the mistress, and/or the mistress herself.
*La regla de regalos* – The rule of the gifts.

**The Ghost of Ezra Pound in a Station of the Mexico City Metro**
This is a playful homage to Pound's 1913 poem, 'In A Station of the Metro', often cited as the birth of Imagism.

*Cilantro* – Sometimes referred to as Mexican parsley. The leaves and stalks are commonly found in Mexican dishes and salsas. The seeds of this plant are ground up and used as a spice called coriander in the UK.

**Rude Awakening**
*No pasa nada.* (lit.) Nothing happened. – Common reassurance of Mexican mothers to comfort children after falling, being frightened or suffering a minor injury.
*No importa.* – (lit.) I give it no importance. It doesn't matter.
*Si Dios quiere.* If God wishes.
*porque, ya me cansé* – "Because, enough already, I'm tired." These infamous words spoken by Mexico's Attorney General, Jesus Murillo Karam, to end a press conference on the investigation into the disappearance and murder of the forty-

three students of Ayotzinapa, became a national scandal and a symbol of the government's lack of interest in solving the crime. *Los desaparicidos* – The disappeared. On the night of 26 September 2014, students of the Normal School Raúl Isidro Burgos Rural (better known as Ayotzinapa Rural Normal School), a teachers' college in the town of Ayotzinapa, set out to attend a protest. The Iguala Municipal police (under orders from the mayor) intercepted the students. During the confrontation, the police panicked and shot several students without justification. The police arrested the other students to silence the witnesses. They were never seen again and their bodies were never found. It is believed that the police handed over the forty-three students to the Guerros Unidos, a Narco-trafficking gang in league with the mayor and police, and that all forty-three of the missing students were murdered and their bodies burned by the Guerros Unidos. The mayor and dozens of others have been arrested, but have yet to be brought to trial.

**Questions of Translation**
*Incipit vita nova* – Literally, "Here begins the new life." Dante refers to meeting his beloved Beatrice.
*confundido* – confused
*Soy, es para la condición permanente.* – I am, is for the permanent condition.
*Estoy, es para la condición temporal.* – I am, is for the temporary condition.
*Dolor* – pain
*Franz Boas* was a German-American scientist, often called the "Father of Modern Anthropology".
*Sufrimiento* – suffering.
*la curva perfecta de su espalda* – The perfect curve of your back.
*cómo se dice* – How to say (How do you say)
*contigo* – with you

**II Stage Whispers**
*auf den Brettern, die die Welt bedeuten* – on the boards (the stage) that mean the world [to me]

**Hotel Eden**
The collage referred to – like many works by Joseph Cornell – is a sculpture assembled from found objects and staged inside a small box (38.3 x 39.7 x 12.1 cm). The central figure is a stuffed parrot, which appears to be caged inside the box and connected with thread or wire to other objects. Made in 1945, it is in the permanent collection of the national Gallery of Canada. If you follow the links below you will find more information about Cornell's work.
https://www.gallery.ca/collection/artwork/the-hotel-eden
https://en.wikipedia.org/wiki/Joseph_Cornell
http://claireelizabethburton.blogspot.com/2008/03/joseph-cornell-collagereality.html

**Odysseus – Isis – Osiris**
The poem refers to and combines ideas from two mythical journeys: the familiar story of the Odyssey and the well-known Egyptian story of Isis and Osiris. Osiris, the god-king of ancient Egypt was murdered and dismembered by his jealous brother Set. Isis (wife and sister of Osiris) travels down the Nile, across all of Egypt to find and reassemble all the pieces of her beloved Osiris and restore him to life.

**Actaeon** – In Greek myth, the hunter, Actaeon, stumbled upon the goddess Artemis bathing and saw her naked body. When she saw him watching her she turned him into a stag and he was chased down and killed by his own hounds.

**IV**

*Ubi nihil vales, ibi nihil velis.* – Often translated as, "Where you are worth nothing, there you should seek nothing"; or, "Where you have no power, you should not try to exert your will." – Samuel Beckett cited this as a favorite phrase, and an important influence on his thinking.

**What Is Your Favourite Colour**
*ADHD –* stands for attention deficit hyperactivity disorder. It is a medical condition. The term is frequently used by parents and teachers to describe any very active student who is a behaviour challenge.

**The Sound of the Sea is the Answer**
*Ceviche* – a popular seafood dish served throughout Mexico and the Americas. Originally from Peru, ceviche is typically made from fresh raw fish cured in citrus juices, such as lemon or lime, and spiced with ají, chili peppers or other seasonings including chopped onions, salt, and cilantro.

**Meeting Again After a Long Time** – The form of this poem (four lines of five syllables each) is taken from the T'ang dynasty quatrain form known as "jueju".

**After a Foolish Argument** – In North America, the black, brown, and grizzly bears eat blackberries.

V

**Semana Santa** – Between 1846 and 1989 US military forces invaded Mexico, and the various countries of Central America and the Caribbean, twenty-seven times. An additional forty-five coups, uprisings and invasions were staged by US-funded mercenaries and paramilitary forces.

The current Central American refugee problem is directly related to this almost continuous interference by US corporations and the military forces acting on their behalf. The puppet régimes installed by the USA have ruled Central America as de facto "company towns" for the benefit of the foreign corporations and the richest one percent of the local population, who collaborate with them.

Local police, politicians and judges are routinely on the corporation payrolls. When those corporations illegally seize land from small farmers and indigenous villages the locals have no recourse. Murder and intimidation are the norm in these countries.

See Mark Rosenfelder, 'U.S. Interventions in Latin America' 1996, at: https://www.zompist.com/latam.html

See also, Mark Tseng-Putterman, 'A Century of U.S. Intervention Created the Immigration Crisis', Jun 21, 2018: https://medium.com/s/story/timeline-us-intervention-central-america-a9bea9ebc148

One of the most scandalous and well-publicized of these murders occurred in 1980. Oscar Romero, the Archbishop of El Salvador, had repeatedly spoken out against the widespread injustice. Romero was murdered on the altar as he said mass. Despite evidence linking several Salvadoran military officers to the crime no one was ever brought to trial for the murder.

For an article on the murder of Archbishop Romero, see: https://www.theguardian.com/theguardian/2000/mar/23/features 11.g21

**Holy Saturday** – Father Jerome Cypher.
For an article reporting the death of Fr. Jerome Cypher, see: https://www.nytimes.com/1975/07/19/archives/inquiry-in-honduras-uncovers-death-of-7-honduras-inquiry-uncovers.html

**VI**

**No Foreign Objects**
*Odysseus' oar* – In order make peace with Poseidon, the god of the sea, the prophet Tiresias instructed Odysseus to take an oar from his ship and walk inland until he found people who knew nothing of the sea, and could not recognize an oar. There, Odysseus was to offer sacrifice to Poseidon, so that he could return home at last.

**Last Candle**
*Münster* – archaic German word for an important church; derived from Latin "monasterium" (monastery). In British English, it corresponds to the word "minster."

**Poco a poco** – Little by little. Also, by and by.

**At the Edge**
*King Jaguar Paw – Mayan name Toh Chak Ich'ak* (died 378) was a much-celebrated king of the Maya city of Tikal. He reigned from 360 until his death in 378, when Tikal was conquered by invaders from the Teotihuacan empire in central Mexico.

# Advance Comments

**These poems are a nectar** that Hamilton, a world citizen and grounded poet of this earth, has gathered for us from Central America, Asia, the Pacific Northwest, and the granite beast of America. *The Hummingbird Sometimes Flies Backward* demonstrates craft steeped in compassion, wit, sorrow, mercy and love. Read, 'A Handful of Idiots', one of many poems where, if we share this poet's honesty, we can recognize ourselves. Drink your fill here, from poems celebrating humanity in the face of global, inhuman, greed. Poems of our deepest heart, they'll fly you in grand directions.
—**Michael Daley, founder of Empty Bowl, author of** *True Heresies*

**Hamilton's long-awaited collection** is a life's work in miniature, taking us from Mexican vistas, Wisconsin farms, ancient ruins and urban jungles in its evocation of the poet's quest for his own truth. Ranging across spiritual, political and erotic sensibilities, these poems are meditative, richly allusive, with frequent, unexpected turns to the ironic, and with a lyrical voice that envelops, sucking you gradually into the vortex of language, metaphor and lived experience.
—**Jason Eng Hun Lee, Hong Kong Baptist University, author of** *Beds In the East.*

**Among other virtues** good poems transmit empathy; their mood and language are uncommon because poetry is uncommon, but the voice that speaks to us, the readers, is ordinary, universal, empathetic. The experiences may be deeply personal, but at the same time they are instantly recognisable, and speak with truth about what it is to be human. Just such poems are contained in this profound, passionate and knowing collection of "world" poems that speak to us in a highly original yet common man's voice.

Ranging between the agricultural land of his early-life home in the American Mid-West, to the rich but transformative experiences of myth-laden and civilisation-spawning Mexico, to the ancient wisdom of Greek mythology, this remarkable collection takes the reader on a compelling journey of the imagination, transcending time and space boundaries at will; the language is in turn lyrical, beautiful, harsh, and as brutal as the pain and crimes against humanity that some of his poems rage against.

The job of poetry according to Hamilton is, "to know the secret names of things and bring the wild sounds/ hidden in darkness together/ into the light." Only by naming with the right words can the poet accomplish this task. This is exactly what the author has achieved with great distinction in this illuminating and exhilarating collection of poems.

**—Michael Ingham, Lingnan University, Hong Kong, author of *Hong Kong – A Cultural and Literary History*.**


**The new Oxford Professor of Poetry**, Alice Oswald, has said of American poetry, "A poem by Ashbery, Jorie Graham or Dickinson exposes the pauses in the brain, articulates indecision…I find that invigorating. British poets put thoughts into their poems but they pour them in as if the poem is a container. Something about the American line just incorporates thinking in verse." She would do well to add another name to her list – D.J. Hamilton.

Section IV of his poetry collection, *The Hummingbird Sometimes Flies Backwards*, is entitled, "Futile Prayers and Awkward Questions" – the second phrase is a telling aspect of Hamilton's poetry. In, 'The Pearl Diver's Mistress', the narrator is constantly questioning and probing until he arrives at moments of insight only to further qualify and refine them. Detached refrain lines are sometimes used to underscore meaning but are often at odds with what has been said. This reminded me of the jabbing, interrogating refrains in Yeats' late ballads; in, 'Parque México', the refrain, "We are all running" (and variations on it), is a good example.

The reader will find Hamilton has a powerful descriptive sense – closely observed landscapes and people – as well as a wide geographical range (Wisconsin to Mexico) and tonal range (contemplative to comic verse).

There are tender love poems that are sure-footed and follow the contour of authenticity, for instance, in the

Shakespearean, 'If All of Life, Were But One Week…'. Sometimes these take a pithy haiku form such as, 'Meeting Again After a Long Time' – "I miss the/we, that we once were."

A number of poems offer self-reflection mediated through the Spanish-language. This is a subtle device to 'translate' the ambiguities and insights of experience in these poems. The traditional tools of poetry – rhyme, alliteration, assonance – are in evidence but are deployed sparingly and strategically. For example, in the poem, 'Actaeon', assonance is used unobtrusively and effectively: "between a sigh and a groan, a sound like a cyclone of desire". The ten-part narrative poem, 'In Ruins', with its metaphoric variations – leaf-cutter ants – is a significant achievement.

R. S. Thomas claimed that poetry arrives at the intellect by way of the heart. The poet's task is to find the effective middle ground. Too much feeling leads to sentimentality; if the poem is too cerebral it may be lifeless. Hamilton's poetry exemplifies how to get this just right!

**—Peter Kennedy, University of Hong Kong, author of *There*.**

# POETRY PUBLISHED BY PROVERSE HONG KONG IN ENGLISH

*Alphabet* by Andrew Simpson Guthrie
*Astra and Sebastian* by L.W. Illsley (*Teenage epic*)
*The Bliss of Bewilderment* by Birgit Bunzel Linder
*The Burning Lake* by Jonathan Locke Hart
*Celestial Promise* by Hayley Ann Solomon
*Chasing Light* by Patricia Glinton-Meicholas
*China Suite and other poems* by Gillian Bickley
*For The Record And Other Poems Of Hong Kong* by Gillian Bickley
*Frida Kahlo's Cry And Other Poems* by Laura Solomon
*Heart to Heart: Poems* by Patty Ho
*Home, Away, Elsewhere* by Vaughan Rapatahana
*The Hummingbird Sometimes Flies Backwards* by D. J. Hamilton
*Immortelle and Bhandaaraa Poems* by Lelawattee Manoo-Rahming.
*In Vitro* by Laura Solomon
*Irreverent Poems For Pretentious People* by Henrik Hoeg
*The Layers Between* by Celia Claase (*Collection of poems and essays*)
*Life Lines* by Shahilla Shariff
*Moving House and Other Poems* by Gillian Bickley
*Of Leaves and Ashes* by Patty Ho
*Of Symbols Misused* by Mary-Jane Newton
*Over the Years* by Gillian Bickley
*Painting the Borrowed House: Poems* by Kate Rogers
*Perceptions* by Gillian Bickley
*Rain on the Pacific Coast* by Elbert Siu Ping Lee
*Refrain* by Jason S Polley
*Savage Charm* by Ahmed Elbeshlawy
*Shadow Play* by James Norcliffe
*Shadows in Deferment* by Birgit Bunzel Linder
*Shifting Sands* by Deepa Vanjani
*Sightings: a collection of Poetry* by Gillian Bickley

*Smoked Pearl* by Akin Jeje
*To Eastern Lands* by Roger Uren
*Unlocking* by Mary-Jane Newton
Violet by Carolina Ilica
*Wonder, Lust & Itchy Feet* by Sally Dellow
The Year of the Apparitions by José Manuel Sevilla
(scheduled, 2020)

## INTERNATIONAL PROVERSE POETRY PRIZE ANTHOLOGIES
*Mingled Voices* ed Gillian and Verner Bickley
*Mingled Voices 2* ed Gillian and Verner Bickley
*Mingled Voices 3* ed Gillian and Verner Bickley

## POETRY IN CHINESE
*Moving House and Other Poems* by Gillian Bickley (in
Chinese with additional contents & b/w photographs)

## EDUCATIONAL
### (English Language)
*Poems to Enjoy, Book 1* by Verner Bickley (3$^{rd}$ Ed) w. 1 audio
CD (Graded poetry anthology w. teaching and learning notes,
glossary, etc.)
*Poems to Enjoy, Book 2* by Verner Bickley (3$^{rd}$ Ed) w. 2 audio
CDs (Graded poetry anthology w. teaching and learning notes,
glossary, etc.)
*Poems to Enjoy, Book 3* by Verner Bickley (3$^{rd}$ Ed) w. 2 audio
CDs (Graded poetry anthology w. teaching and learning notes,
glossary, etc.)
*Poems to Enjoy, Book 4* by Verner Bickley (3$^{rd}$ Ed) w. 2 audio
CDs (Graded poetry anthology w. teaching and learning notes,
glossary, etc.)
*Poems to Enjoy, Book 5* by Verner Bickley (3$^{rd}$ Ed) w. 3 audio
CDs (Graded poetry anthology w. teaching and learning notes,
glossary, etc.)

9 789888 491711